STORY OF THE NILE

ILLUSTRATED BY STEVE NOON
WRITTEN BY DR. ANNE MILLARD

DORLING KINDERSLEY

London • New York • Munich • Melbourne • Delhi

CONTENTS

**LONDON, NEW YORK, MUNICH,
MELBOURNE, AND DELHI**

Editors Zahavit Shalev, Linda Esposito,
and Christine Heilman
Designer Diane Thistlethwaite
Production Linda Dare
Jacket design Christopher Branfield

First American Edition, 2003

Published in the United States by
DK Publishing, Inc. 375 Hudson Street
New York, New York 10014
03 04 05 06 07 08 10 9 8 7 6 5 4 3 2 1

Copyright © 2003 Dorling Kindersley Limited

All rights reserved under International and Pan-American
Copyright Conventions. No part of this publication may be
reproduced, stored in a retrieval system, or transmitted in any
form or by any means, electronic, mechanical, photocopying,
recording or otherwise, without the prior written permission of
the copyright owner. Published in Great Britain
by Dorling Kindersley Limited.

A catalog record for this book is available
from the Library of Congress.

ISBN 0-7894-9871-5

Color reproduction by Dot Gradations, UK
Printed and bound in Singapore by Tien Wah Press

Discover more at
www.dk.com

THE STORY OF THE NILE

Take a journey along some 4,350 miles (7,000 km) from the source of the Nile to the Mediterranean Sea. At its source, the river is called the White Nile. We follow its course across plains full of game, through rocky gorges and tropical forests, and into an impenetrable swamp. At the site of the modern city of Khartoum, it merges with another river, the Blue Nile. Then nature plays a trick. For the last 1,120 miles (1,800 km) of its journey, the Nile flows through a desert!

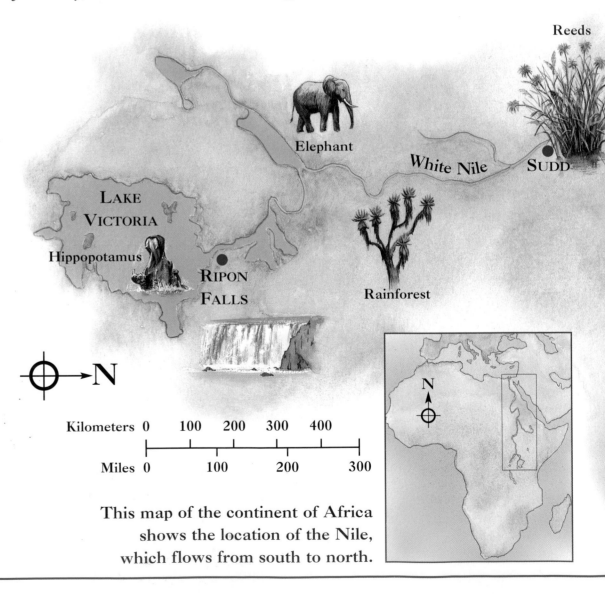

This map of the continent of Africa shows the location of the Nile, which flows from south to north.

Finally, the river divides into several channels, flowing through the rich farmland of the Delta into the Mediterranean Sea. However, each year, when the melting snow and the spring rains in the mountains of Ethiopia surge down the Blue Nile and into the Nile River, the river north of Khartoum floods. These life-giving waters gave birth to one of the world's oldest civilizations, and they continue to make life possible for the modern nations in the region today.

Our guide on this journey is a magic pelican, flying through time as well as space. Through him, we will see how the Nile has influenced all aspects of the life of its people, and witness some of the epic events that took place during its long history. We'll see the great kingdoms that flourished along its banks, and the ordinary people who have relied on the mighty Nile for their survival.

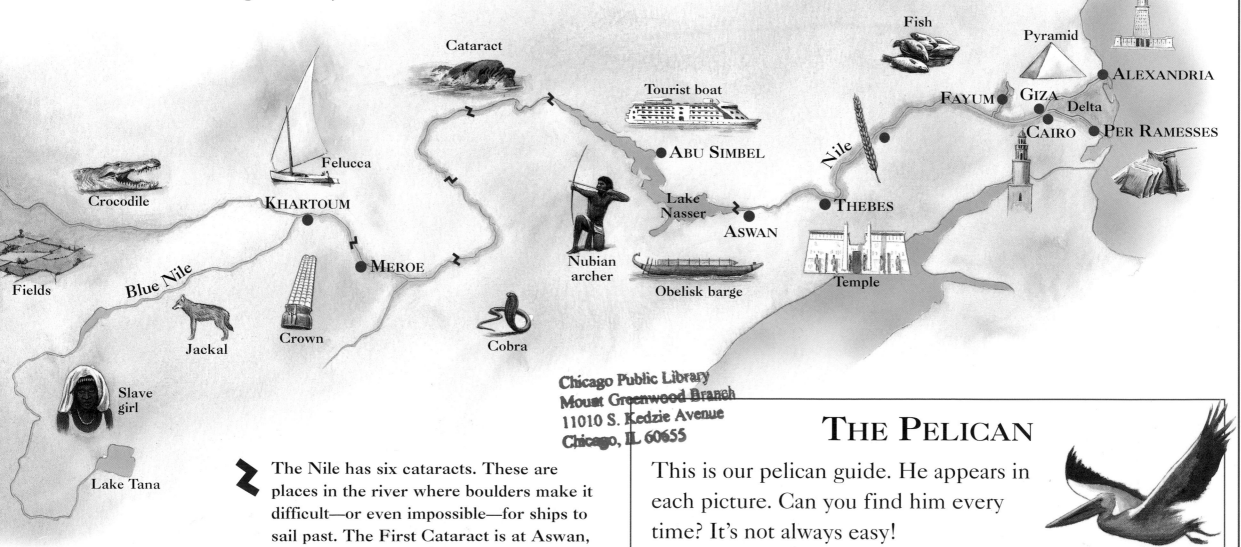

Cataract

Fish

Pyramid

Tourist boat

ALEXANDRIA

FAYUM GIZA Delta

Felucca

ABU SIMBEL

Nile

CAIRO PER RAMESSES

Crocodile

KHARTOUM

Lake Nasser

THEBES

Nubian archer

ASWAN

MEROE

Fields

Blue Nile

Obelisk barge

Temple

Jackal

Crown

Cobra

Slave girl

Lake Tana

Z The Nile has six cataracts. These are places in the river where boulders make it difficult—or even impossible—for ships to sail past. The First Cataract is at Aswan, the Sixth near Khartoum.

THE PELICAN

This is our pelican guide. He appears in each picture. Can you find him every time? It's not always easy!

THE SOURCE OF THE NILE
Ripon Falls, Lake Victoria, July 28, 1862 AD

Englishman John Speke stands by Lake Victoria and watches its waters spill into the Nile. Many explorers have set out to discover the source of the River Nile, but none have succeeded until now. Speke names the 66-ft- (142-m-) wide waterfall the Ripon Falls.

Lionesses

Thompson's gazelles

Goliath heron

Wildebeest

Zebra

Hartebeest

Ripon Falls

Rainbow

Hippopotamuses

Fish eagle

Find the fishermen trying to escape from some angry hippopotamuses.

Where do the local villagers wash their clothes?

4

The head guide, Sidi Bombay, is in charge of the porters. He is paid 60 dollars a year. A palisade around their village protects the people and their cattle from wild animals.

Storks

Village

Thatched houses

Lake Victoria

Gathering firewood

Cattle

Washing clothes

Fisherman

Fish

Building shelter

Getting water

Harpooning fish

John Speke's tent

Porters

Crocodiles

John Speke

Sidi Bombay

Preparing food

Find the Goliath heron. It is the largest heron in the world. Two hungry lionesses are on the lookout for food. Can you see them?

 The local people make a living by farming, as well as fishing. The lake has a good supply of fish, which are carried over the falls. This makes a fisherman's job easy!

THE WORLD'S BIGGEST SWAMP
The Sudd, *c.* 62 AD

The Nile flows north through changing scenery of lush tropical forest and grassy plains. Then it enters a vast swamp called the Sudd, which is more than 400 miles (650 km) long. There are only three channels through the Sudd, and all are infested with snakes, crocodiles, and insects. Emperor Nero has sent a scouting party to look for new lands to conquer south of Egypt, but the Sudd is proving too much even for these tough Roman soldiers.

Local fisherman

Drying fish

Dragonfly

Insects

Boatmen

Slaves

Doctor

Stores

Centurions

Crested crane

Soldiers

6

How many crocodiles can you see?

The slaves that the Romans have brought along come from all over the Roman Empire.

The swamp is a breeding ground for malaria-carrying mosquitoes. Who is feeling ill?

Which soldier is afraid of snakes?

Flamingos

Spoonbill

Swallows

Shoebill

Cobra

Shields

Slave from Britain

Slave

Crocodile

7

SLAVE CITY

Khartoum, *c.* 1840 AD

The Blue Nile, which begins in Ethiopia, flows into the White Nile at Khartoum. When the Egyptians conquered northern Sudan in 1821, they made this village their headquarters. Khartoum is now a rich trading city. People come from far and wide to buy its main commodities—slaves and elephant tusks for the ivory trade.

Feluccas

Mud-brick house

Unloading ivory

Wealthy Egyptian

European explorers

Basket-maker

European artist

Haggling

Find the pelican. Who is after him?

European and American traders come to Khartoum to buy ivory for luxury goods.

Slave hunters are licensed by the Egyptians to capture anyone they can within a huge area around Sudan.　African slaves are brought down the White Nile from the south.

East bank

Minaret

Blue Nile

White Nile

European traders

Ethiopian slave girls

Slave dealer

Coffee shop

Hookah pipe

Bidding for slaves

Guard

Slaves

Slave

Master

Egyptian soldiers

Beautiful girls have been torn from their families in Ethiopia to be sold in Khartoum.　Spot the local "carryout."

Around 50,000 slaves a year are sold by auction in this busy Khartoum market.　The majority of Egyptians are Muslims. They have built mosques as places of worship.

KINGDOM OF GOLD
The Royal City of Meroe, *c*. 50 AD

Meroe lies between the Third and Sixth Nile Cataracts. It grew out of the land called Kush by the Egyptians, who once ruled much of it and whose influence can still be felt. Meroe is immensely wealthy. One writer tells us that even the prisoners have gold chains! This audience in the palace courtyard is being held to celebrate a military victory.

Egyptian-style buildings

Giraffe

Indian traders

African traders

Spices

Incense burner

Iron sword and spear

King's warrior

Nubian prisoners

Courtiers

High priest

Priestess

10

Can you spot the bust of the Roman emperor?   Some uninvited spectators are getting a terrific view. Can you spot them?

Meroe attracts traders from many lands because of its gold, iron, cotton, and exotic animals.

Elephants are tamed and used in war, as well as in royal processions.

In Meroe, large ladies are much admired. Can you spot the powerful "queen mother" giving advice to her son, the king?

Egyptian-style crowns

King

Queen mother

Nile

Queen

Roman senator

Roman soldiers

Princess

Courtiers

Ethiopian traders

Royal nurse

Princess

Princes

Precious spices

Fan bearer

King's pet leopard

Gold and silver

Rome is interested in Meroe's wealth. A visiting senator is presenting some horses to the king as a gift.

The king shows off his wealth and power to foreign visitors.

11

BORDER FORT

Nubia, *c.* 1850 BC

The Nile has been used to carry soldiers and supplies for thousands of years. Since conquering Nubia, the Egyptians have built huge forts to protect their new frontier. Nubia is rich in gold, copper, and precious stones, so the forts are also important trading centers. A new governor is arriving to take over at this fort.

Can you spot who almost stood on a snake?

New soldiers are arriving by boat to begin a tour of duty at the fort.

Vultures

Nubian village

Soldiers' barges

Nile

Grain barge

Governor's furniture

Local traders

Governor's hunting dogs

Governor and wife

Guard of honor

Donkeys

Guard

Army patrol

Officer

12

The fort can be approached either by river or by land. A well-defended land gate reduces the risk of an attack. This caravan is taking goods north to Egypt.

Fort cattle

Soldiers' families

Donkey caravan

Scribes

Guard dog

Kushite spies

Lizard

Jerboa

Many archers in the Egyptian army come from Nubia, which the Egyptians call "Land of the Bow."   These spies come from the warlike Kingdom of Kush, south of Nubia.

TOURISTS AT THE TEMPLES
Abu Simbel, present day

In 1971 the Egyptian government opened the High Dam. As the waters built up south of it, Nubia drowned under Lake Nasser, the biggest artificial lake in the world. Before the dam opened, a huge rescue operation was mounted to save Nubia's ancient monuments. Some of the great temples, like these at Abu Simbel, were cut up into thousands of blocks and rebuilt on higher ground.

Ramesses II's temple

Statues of Ramesses

Tour groups

Egyptian guide

Selling guidebooks

Postcard seller

Filming

Tourist boat

14

 Can you spot the group of tourists who are all wearing the same hats? Tourism is very important to Egypt's economy.

Ramesses built a temple for his favourite wife, Nefertari.   Ramesses fathered almost two hundred children. Some are represented by statues outside the temple.

Nefertari's temple

Selling sun hats

Temple guardian with key

Selling cold drinks

Nile (Lake Nasser)

Police boat

The dam exists to make sure Egypt has a regular water supply.

Ramesses built the most monuments of any pharaoh.

15

The temples were carved out of the mountain and took four years to move.   Mass tourism began in 1869, when Thomas Cook began organizing trips to Egypt.

EGYPT'S HIGHWAY
Aswan, *c.* 1500 BC

The quickest and easiest way to move people and heavy goods is on the river. The best time to take stone from quarries to building projects is between July and October, when the Nile comes closest to the quarries while flooding all the flat farmland between the desert cliffs. Here, a giant barge carries obelisks from the Aswan granite quarries north to the Karnak temple in Thebes.

Temple of Khnum

Elephantine Island

Obelisk

Boat wrecks

Royal messenger's boat

Senmut's barge

Cattle barge

Noble lady

Huntsmen

Steward

Noble in chariot

Wine

Scribe

Servant

16

Can you find the man who has fallen overboard?

Rich people can afford to be carried, but everyone else walks.

Former governors of Aswan are buried in tombs in the desert cliffs.

The Temple of Khnum, the god responsible for the annual flooding, is on Elephantine Island.

Nobles' tombs

Fishing boats

Boats towing barge

Nubian archers

Steering oar

Grain barge

Ferry

Housewife

Housewives come to the river to get water and do their laundry.

Can you see what a naughty monkey has just done?

Chariots are used for battle and for hunting in the desert.

The rocks and the fast-flowing rapids of the First Cataract at Aswan pose a danger to ships.

THE FEAST OF OPET

Thebes, c. 1180 BC

The Nile is so important in the daily lives of ancient Egyptians that it also features significantly in their religious beliefs. Here in Thebes, a great river procession is bringing the statue of the god Amun from his main temple at Karnak to his second temple to celebrate his life-giving powers. The festival is called Opet. It lasts for eleven days and attracts great crowds.

Ibis

Entrance to temple

White walls

Obelisk

Statue of Ramesses II

Flagpole

Fan bearers

Statues of sacred baboons

Libyan captives

Ramesses III

Spot four ways to get a better view of the procession.

Outside the temple stand Ramesses III and his queen.

18

At festivals, some people are overcome by religious excitement. The temple walls are dazzling. They are painted white and covered with pictures of kings and gods.

Cliffs

Pilgrims' boats

Funeral procession

Amun's barge

Priests

Shrine

High priest

Priestesses Petitioner

Musicians

Dancers

Offerings

Guards

Ibises and baboons are sacred to Thoth, the god of wisdom. When statues of gods have to be moved, they are put in shrines on small boats and carried by priests.

A reed shelter provides welcome shade during a break from work in the fields.

 Threshing is a simple technique that breaks the grains of wheat free from their stalks.

EVERY LAST DROP
Middle Egypt, *c.* 1560 AD

Since Egypt has so little rain, water for crops comes from the Nile. Ancient Egyptians discovered how to catch the floodwater each year and carry it in canals and ditches around their fields. The Arabs who conquered Egypt use the same system. Like their ancestors, these peasants grow grain, flax, vegetables, and fruit.

Washing clothes

Felucca

Camel

Date palms

Shaduf

Cattle

Can you find the nasty boy bullying his younger brother?

Somebody has to climb the tree to get to the ripe dates.

20

 A would-be tomb robber is out of luck—the tombs have already been robbed, 3,000 years ago!

 The shaduf and the water wheel both raise the water to a higher level.

During winnowing, the chaff—the light outer casing of each grain—is blown away. All Muslims try to make a pilgrimage at least once to the holy city of Mecca.

Church

Goats

Muezzin

Flax

Christian
ceremony

Ancient tombs

Mosque

Pigeon lofts

Wheat

Pilgrims

Oven

Funeral
procession

Canal

Carpenters

Potter

Water
wheel

Chickens

Outdoors, all women wear black clothes that cover them completely.

Who has broken in to the cabbage patch?

Grilled pigeon is a delicacy eaten on special occasions.   A muezzin calls people to prayer. Most Egyptians converted from Christianity to Islam when the Arabs invaded.

THE GIFTS OF THE NILE

The Fayum, *c.* 1890 BC

Water for drinking, bathing, and watering crops comes from the Nile. The river provides a plentiful supply of fish and wild birds to eat, as well as reeds that can be made into anything from boats to paper. To this elderly nobleman and his family, sports and relaxation are other gifts of the Nile.

Palm trees

Building a reed boat

Bundles of reeds

Collecting water

Hippo hunting

Spear-fishing

Birds caught in net

Bird catchers

Servant

Nobleman's eldest son

Wife

Daughter

Pied kingfisher

Reed boat

Lotus

Can you spot the children playing with toy boats?

The pelican has had a lucky escape from a net. Can you see him?

22

People do their laundry in the river, and also come here to get water. Boats can be made of wood or reeds. Reed boats are light and particularly good for sports.

Pyramid

Papyrus reeds

Fishing

Cutting reeds

Washing clothes

Water joust

Pet monkey

Steersman

Nurse

Daughter

Nurse

Nobleman

Shield

Sailors

Playing flute

Oars

Steering oar

Wife

Servant

Picnic

Plumb line

Wooden boat

Son

Exotic animals like monkeys are imported from lands farther south. The lotus is a sacred flower. How many can you count?

23

Can you see the young boy swimming? His nurse is terrified because the river is full of crocodiles! Egyptians drink a lot of beer. Nobles often sip theirs through a straw.

THE FUNERAL OF KING KHUFU

Giza, *c.* 2500 BC

This is the funeral of King Khufu. The sun and the river are central to daily life in Egypt, so they also shape people's ideas about the afterlife. The Egyptians believe that their king is the son of Re, the sun god, who journeys through the underworld Kingdom of the Dead at night. Khufu's body is being ferried over the Nile to the west bank where the sun sets. It will be laid to rest inside a huge pyramid whose shape reflects the sun's rays.

Egyptians believe the sky god, Horus, can visit earth as a falcon. Can you see one?

Can you spot the new king and queen?

Pyramid of King Khufu

Pyramids for the three queens

Falcon

Small palace

Mortuary temple

Causeway

Offerings of food and animals

Statue

Royal bodyguards

Trained mourners

Funeral boat

Harbor

Egrets

24

The funeral boats are buried near to the pyramids so that King Khufu can sail alongside the sun in the afterlife. Women mourners wail and splash their faces with mud.

Can you see the children who have sneaked in to get a good view?

Can you see Khafra sulking because he is not the new king?

Pigeons

Date palms

Valley temple

Priestesses with sistrums and flowers

New king and queen

Coffin placed on model boat

Soldiers

Noblemen and women mourners

Lector priest reading prayers

High priest

Royal family

Chief queen

Prince Khafra

25

A ceremony in the mortuary temple gives the dead king back all his bodily senses. The chief queen is the most important wife. Her sons are first in line for the throne.

A HERO SETS OUT

Cairo, c. 1190 AD

Here, the great Muslim leader Salah el Din, or Saladin, sets off to fight the Christian armies in the Third Crusade. After the Muslim Arabs had conquered Egypt in 640 AD, they built Cairo at the place where the Nile divides into several channels, and made it their capital. A great fortress—the Citadel—built on a rocky outcrop protects the city.

Camel caravan

Dancing girls

Barber

Goats

Nubian maid

Snake charmer

Soldiers

Saladin

26

Wooden grilles on windows give the women indoors privacy. Egyptians have been producing decorative furniture featuring inlaid strips of wood for thousands of years.

Citadel

Mosque

Minaret

Bathhouse

Aqueduct

Wooden balcony

Furniture

Spices

Shoes

Textiles

Scribe

Rugs

Copper

Beggar

Bedouin

Water seller

27

Cairo is built from blocks that belonged to the pyramids in Giza.

Can you see who is throwing a flower to Saladin?

The Crusades are being fought by Muslims and Christians for control of the Holy Land.   Arab traders do business as far away as central Asia and China.

INTERNATIONAL RELATIONS
Per Ramesses, *c.* 1260 BC

Diplomats and traders always use the Nile when they come to do business in Egypt. This is the new city of Per Ramesses, built by King Ramesses II on an eastern branch of the Nile. Its location allows the King to keep an eye on his great rivals, the Hittites, who want to take over Egypt's eastern empire.

Egyptian warship

Nubian ship

Imported timber

Beer shop

Oil

Ambassador from Mycenae

Grain

Medjay

Scribe

Canaanite traders from Byblos

Local ship

Ivory

Foreman

Can you see how a woman is carrying her baby?

Egyptians do not mind foreigners worshipping their own gods.

28

Bedouins live in desert regions, moving around with their flocks between watering holes.

Egyptian officials are welcoming the new ambassador from Mycenae and his wife.

Pylon gate under construction

Habiru slaves

Mud-brick city wall

Decorated gateway

Imported horses

Ostrich feathers

Canaanite shrine

Dancer and musician

Wine

Hittite spies

Watermelons

Libyans

Hittite woman with bodyguard

Thief

Bedouin from Sinai

Nubians

Grain from Egypt is exported all over the eastern Mediterranean.

After fighting the Hittites, Ramesses finally makes peace with them in the twenty-first year of his reign.

29

STUDENTS AND STREET FIGHTS

Alexandria, *c.* 90 BC

Founded on the orders of Alexander the Great, who conquered Egypt in 332 BC, Alexandria is a fabulously wealthy city, and its Mouseion is a world-famous center of learning. Greeks, Egyptians, and Jews live here. The Greeks are rowdy, rioting when anything displeases them. A king will later be killed by a rioting mob.

Temple

Lighthouse

Courtyard

Romans escaping

Students

Lictor

Greek rioters

Romans

Can you see who is hanging out their laundry?

Ships as far as 30 miles (50 km) away can see the lighthouse.

Isis is currently Egypt's most popular goddess.

Can you see a shop owner and her dog fighting back against the rioters?

Mouseion

Harbor

Mediterranean Sea

Jetty

Theater

Palace

School

Patient being bled

Barber

Selling medicines

Fountain house

Jewish wedding party

High Priestess

King

Isis

High Priest

Guards

Priests

Greek soldiers

31

EGYPTIAN TIMELINE |P24-25| |P22-23| |P12-13| |P16-17| |P28-29| |P18-19| |P30-31|

| 3200 BC | 3000 | Pharaohs rule | 2500 | 2000 | 1390 1850 | 1500 | 1260 1180 | 1000 | 600 | 323 | Greeks rule | 90 30 | BC |

Egypt becomes one kingdom | Alexander conquers Egypt | Rome conquers Egypt

GLOSSARY

Alexander the Great—(356–323 BC) King of Macedon, conqueror of an empire that reached as far as India. After he died, his generals divided his empire between them. Ptolemy became king of Egypt and his descendants ruled until 30 BC, when Egypt was conquered by Rome.

Arabs—People from the Arabian Peninsula. They conquered a vast empire in the Middle East that included Egypt.

Aswan Dam—This holds the waters of the Nile's annual flood and drives turbines that produce Egypt's electricity. It was opened in 1970.

Bedouins—Nomadic, desert-dwelling people who wander with their flocks. Some are also traders.

Blue Nile—River that flows from Lake Tana in the Ethiopian highlands into the White Nile near Khartoum, thus forming the Nile River.

Britain—Former colonial power. It became involved in Egypt because the Suez Canal provided a quicker route to India, which was part of the British Empire. Britain administered Egypt as a Protectorate from 1882 to 1922.

Christians—Followers of Jesus Christ. Egypt was officially a Christian country from 391 AD to 640 AD.

Delta—Triangle-shaped area between modern Cairo and the Mediterranean Sea. The Nile divides at Cairo into several channels that flow through the Delta, making it a rich farming area.

Fayum—Area of rich land southwest of modern Cairo. Its great lake was partially drained by Middle Kingdom kings to reclaim land for farming.

Habiru—An Egyptian word referring to slaves. Biblical Hebrews may have been among these enslaved peoples.

Karnak—The larger of the god Amun's two temples in Thebes. The smaller one is now called Luxor.

Khartoum—The capital of Sudan.

Khufu—One of the kings of Egypt. He built the largest of all the pyramids. Two of the seven boats buried in pits around his pyramid have survived. The one thought to have carried his body to the pyramid has been restored and is displayed in its own museum in Giza.

Kush—Land between the Third and Fifth Cataracts conquered by Egypt. Kush broke free of Egyptian rule in about 1000 BC and founded its own kingdom with Nubia. Around 750–663 BC, Kushite kings ruled Egypt.

Lictor—Member of a ceremonial guard for Roman officials. Lictors carried fasces—axes surrounded by bundles of rods—signifying their power.

Lighthouse—Tall building with a fire or light on top to guide ships to port. The lighthouse of Alexandria was one of the Seven Wonders of the World. It was completed in 280 BC. Earthquakes destroyed it in the 14th century AD, and stone from it was used to build a fort.

Luxor—Smaller of the god Amun's temples in Thebes.

Mamelukes—Slaves who had been trained as soldiers. They overthrew their masters, the Ayyibids, and ruled Egypt 1250–1517 AD.

Meroe—A rich African kingdom whose culture was important from *c.* 600 BC to 200 AD. It was finally overthrown by the King of Axum (in what is now Ethiopia) *c.* 300 AD.

Middle Kingdom—The period from about 2040 BC to 1650 BC. During this time the Kings built pyramids near the Fayum. The other two great periods of Egyptian history were the Old Kingdom, when the pyramids at Giza were built, and the New Kingdom, when Egypt conquered a great empire.

Mouseion—Center of scholarship in Alexandria that was created to honor the Muses (goddesses of learning).

Muezzin—Person who calls Muslims to prayers. He stands in a minaret, a tower adjoining the mosque.

Muslims—Followers of the Prophet Mohammed (*c.* 570–632 AD), founder of the Islamic faith.

Nubia—Land between the First and Second Cataracts, often ruled by Egypt.

Obelisk—Tall column of stone shaped at the top like a pyramid, a symbol of the sun god, Re. Pairs of obelisks were built in front of temples.

Petitioner—Person asking a god or goddess for advice. A question requiring an answer of "yes" or "no" would be addressed to a statue of the god. If it became so heavy that the priests carrying it sank to the ground, or if it shook, the god was answering "yes."

Pyramid—Tomb for an Egyptian king. The largest is Khufu's at Giza. It was 481 ft (147 m) tall, with sides 746 ft (227 m) long. Two thousand years after the pyramids at Giza were built, the Greeks named them one of the Seven Wonders of the World.

Ramesses II—King of Egypt, 1290–1224 BC. He built many temples and statues, as well as a new capital, Per Ramesses, in the Delta. His main enemies were the Hittites, who lived in what is now Turkey. Many scholars believe he was the king the Bible says enslaved the Hebrews.

Rome—Powerful nation. In the first century BC, the Roman Empire was expanding rapidly. Rome wanted to conquer Egypt because it was wealthy and exported wheat that Rome needed to feed its people.

Saladin—Salah el Din Yusuf Ayyub (1137–1193 AD). He ruled most of the Middle East and fought Richard Lion-Heart during the Third Crusade (1182–1193 AD). His family, the Ayyibids, ruled Egypt until 1250.

Scribe—Person who reads and writes for other people in exchange for a fee.

Shrine—Place holding holy articles.

Sherden—Eastern Mediterranean people who were part of the Sea Peoples who raided Egypt. Ramesses II captured some Sherden and then hired them to fight for him.

Suez Canal—Channel linking the Mediterranean and the Red Sea. It was opened in 1869.

Thebes—Ancient city that the Egyptians called Wast, and the Greeks knew as Thebes. The modern city is called Luxor.

Turks—Muslims from Turkey. In the 16th century AD they ruled a vast empire in the Middle East. They conquered Egypt in 1517 but lost control of it under Mohammed Ali in 1811.

White Nile—River that flows from Lake Victoria through Uganda and into Sudan. At Khartoum it joins the Blue Nile to form the Nile River.

INDEX

|P10-11| |P6-7| |P26-27| |P20-21| |P8-9| |P4-5| |P14-15|

| AD 43 | 50 62 | Romans rule | 300 | 640 | Arabs rule | 1096 | 1190 1250 | Mamelukes rule | 1517 1560 | Turks rule | 1840 1862 | 1952 | 2000 |

Christianity comes to Egypt | Arabs conquer Egypt | Crusades begin | Egypt becomes a Republic